What's Next?

The most important career guide to help you find the right job, be more confident and achieve career success.

Mohamed Hanbal

Copyright © 2017 Mohamed Hanbal

All rights reserved.

ISBN-10: 1544973934
ISBN-13: 978-1544973937

To my wife Anna, my daughter Faridah, my family, and to the memory of my Father who taught me that nothing is impossible.

To all the people around the world who believed in me. If I can do it, you can do it also.

CONTENTS

	Acknowledgments	ix
	Introduction	xi
1	How Do I Know What I Want In Life, Or: What Is My Life Purpose?	1
2	How To Reduce My Fear Of The Future And The Feeling Of Being Inadequate?	9
3	How To Attract A Good Employer Through My CV. And: What If I Do Not Have Good Grades Or Huge Experience?	14
4	Which Questions Should I Expect In An Interview? And: What Can I Ask?	23
5	Where Should I Start My Career? Or In Other Words: In Which Department?	35
6	Should I Work In A Big Multinational Company Or In A Medium-Sized Company?	39
7	What If I Made The Wrong Career Move Or Made A Wrong Decision In My Life In General?	43
8	If I Am Working Inside A Company, What Are The Main Factors That Can Help Me Move Up Faster Within The Same Company?	49
9	How Can I Accelerate My Career Progress In General And Along With It Earn More Money?	54
10	When To Switch My Job Or Department. And: When To Leave The Whole Company?	59

DOWNLOAD THE AUDIOBOOK FOR FREE!

READ THIS FIRST

Just to say thanks for buying my book, I would like to give you the Audiobook version 100% FREE!

Go to:

http://mohamedhanbal.subscribemenow.com

Mohamed Hanbal

ACKNOWLEDGMENTS

I would like to convey my sincere appreciation and to thank all the people who believed in the message of this book and helped in making it reach as many people around the world as possible.

Also, special thanks to:

Anamaria Comanita

Anne Scheiber

Daniel Jambres

Fabiana Canale

Fabian Höft

Jonas Stratmann

Jonas Wagner

Marvin Engel

Mohamed El-Agaty

Nelli Schwabauer

Nermine Nabil

Niclas Zimmermann

Omar Warraky

Theresa Stach

Mohamed Hanbal

What's Next?

Introduction

If you are studying at university and you are one step away from starting your career; or if you just graduated and you are searching for a job and you do not know where to start; or even if you have already started your career but are confused in the middle of all the myths and career advice that you hear all the time - then this book is for you.

I have divided this book into chapters. Each chapter answers a specific question. You do not have to move sequentially through the book. This is a guide that you can keep with you along the way and use when needed. So feel free to either read the chapters in sequence or to go directly to the chapters that you need the most in the current phase of your career journey.

<u>Why should you consider what I wrote in this book?</u>

I know that maybe you will ask yourself, "Why should I listen to him?". And I will try to answer this question as briefly as possible.

In Short:

- I have lived in different countries within 2 continents.
- I have started 2 private businesses.
- I have worked in 3 of the leading multinational companies in the world.
- In different departments such as Engineering, Procurement and Project Management.
- And in 4 different industries including but not limited to Telecommunications and Automotive.
- And I have led global teams in projects with a sales revenue of more than 100 million USD over lifetime.
- I have done business and run projects with customers such as Daimler, BMW, Audi, VW, Bosch, Jaguar Land Rover, Volvo and others.
- I hold an Engineering degree as well as an MBA degree.

And currently, I am a Leadership and Performance Expert, Public Speaking Champion and one of the Top Ten Speakers in the North, Middle and East Europe Championship of Public Speaking 2015. I am also a lecturer at one of the Universities in Germany.

During my career, I had interviews in big reputable companies. Some of these companies are P&G (Procter & Gamble), Orange (France Telecom), and EDC in Egypt. And Daimler, Deutsche Telecom (T-Mobile), TE Connectivity, General Motors-Opel, Delphi and JLG Industries in Germany.

Some of these interviews went very well, and some did not go well. And some of these interviews ended up with a contract and an agreement between me and the employer, and in others either I or the employer rejected an agreement.

However, I was lucky to gather all of these experiences from these interviews and to spot the common patterns. Most importantly, I was able to understand one important fact: If a company is global, the interview questions that you should expect are the same by around 70%, no matter whether you are being interviewed in Europe or in the Middle East. The differences are really minor and can be ignored.

As a lecturer, I interact with a lot of students and fresh graduates who really need help and guidance in order to take the first steps in their careers. I give a lot of speeches to help these students and fresh graduates and I speak to them, and discovered that their questions are almost the same. So I asked myself, "Why couldn't I take the most common questions that students or fresh graduates ask, and create a short book? A book which can take the reader directly to the bottom line?" And accordingly, I wrote this book as a career guide for any student, fresh graduate or career starter in any place in the world. The experiences that I spoke about in the previous paragraphs are now between your hands waiting for you to make the best use of them.

Throughout this book, I refer to employers, managers and others as "him" where of course just as often as not, we are talking about a woman not a man. This is just to make the text flow more easily and does not reflect the gender of the people involved.

What's Next?

One last point. This is not a theory book. So if you are expecting me to write each sentence and back it up with scientific research and sources, then this book is not for you. Of course sometimes I use resources and researches but only when needed. Remember: The aim of this book is to give you the answers that you are searching for in less than two hours of reading.

So welcome on board and let us start this journey together. And if you ever feel that you need to reach out to me to ask me something or to share with me your opinion about the book, then you can always reach me on my email address shown below. I would love to hear from you.

Mohamed Hanbal
Oftersheim, Germany
mohamed@mohamedhanbal.com
Instagram: hanbalmohamed
Facebook Page: @mohamedhanbal2015

Mohamed Hanbal

1 HOW DO I KNOW WHAT I WANT IN LIFE? OR: WHAT IS MY LIFE PURPOSE?

"The two most important days in your life are the day you are born and the day you find out why." – Mark Twain

One day I was standing in a building waiting for the elevator to arrive. During this time, there was already a pregnant lady standing beside me. As we entered the elevator and pressed the required floor button, an old man in his eighties suddenly appeared entering the building's main door, and I saw on his face the desperate look of someone trying to reach the elevator before it goes up; so I immediately stopped and opened the elevator door for him. When he entered the elevator he smiled and said in a very kind and ironic manner: "Thank you so much for helping an old man like me who is useless now in this stage of life and about to die soon".

After I went out of the elevator I could not stop myself from thinking about the whole situation. And even though it is a very normal daily situation, I found my brain connecting a triangle where the three angles of this triangle were the baby who will be born soon and will start his life, me as the middle-aged man, and this old man who feels that his life will end soon. I found my imagination flying and I started asking myself: "If I had the chance to speak with this old man more, what type of advice would he give me at this phase of his life? What type of advice would he give to this newborn baby after he or she is born? Is he happy and satisfied about what he achieved in his life or is there a place deep inside of him where he longs to go back in time in order to change something? Was it my destiny to see the full stages of the human life cycle reflected in the form of the pregnant lady, the old man and me, gathered in an elevator, in order to trigger me to think about what I want to achieve in my life, and to look forward to how I want my ending to be?" All of these questions suddenly popped up in my mind and I could not do anything to stop them.

In Stephen Covey's book "The 7 Habits Of Highly Effective People," one of the habits is "Begin With The End In Mind." As explained in the book,

Covey meant that no matter how much you are busy in your daily life and no matter what you are doing, you have to add a sense of purpose to what you do each day, and this sense of purpose is through having a vision and by keeping your end target of what you are doing in mind. You have to define your required outcome in advance and not only care about getting things done or living each day as it comes. Think about it from this angle and ask yourself: What is my vision? What do I want to reach in life? What do I want my colleagues at work to say about me after I retire or leave my work? What do I want my family and friends to remember about me after I die?

Unfortunately most people jump into their professional lives without asking themselves these questions and without giving themselves a chance to think about what they really want to achieve in their lives.

They graduate from the university and apply directly for several jobs in different departments and different companies with one important goal in their heads which is to start making good money. And as soon as they are accepted in any of them, what do they do? They start spending excessively.

They move to a bigger or a separate apartment. They buy a new car. They live at a higher standard, travel more, spend more; and later they maybe think about buying their own house with a mortgage.

Several years pass by and they discover that they are not feeling fulfilled anymore. In fact, they were feeling more fulfilled in the beginning when they started their careers because it was a new stage of their lives with a lot of things to learn and a lot of things to do and all of this brought momentum to their lives. The transformation from the student life to the professional life was the key. And when their learning curve at their jobs becomes flat, and life moves in one routine, they start feeling that they made the wrong choice and start thinking about changing their lives by doing a career shift such as moving to another department, industry, company, or even start their own business. But unfortunately the first challenge that they face is themselves.

They feel worried that things may not go well in their new job or with their new employer, and they do not want to take this risk because they are already used to a specific standard of living; so they do not want to risk going lower than this standard. "What if I did not succeed in this new job? What if I did not integrate or like my new employer? How can I live at a lower standard than my current one? What would my friends say or think about me?" …and lots of similar questions pop up at the top of their minds. And then comes the most dangerous question: "I am now paying for a mortgage on my new house and I bought my car on a loan, what would happen if I did not like the new job or if I failed? How would I pay my mortgage or loan?" All of these questions stand as a barrier in front of them and the change that they want to make, until they surrender and accept the current status from the perspective that "something that you know or guarantee is far better than the unknown."

Where To Start

When you graduate out of university you have a lot of options in front of you. You can apply and work at a big company. You can also apply and work at a medium-sized or small company. Or maybe you can start your own business. Or you can decide to have a one-year break and go and travel to see the world before you decide anything.

However, no matter what your decision is, please start by asking yourself one question before moving one step forward or deciding anything. "Where do I see myself in five years?" I know you are going to tell me that this is a standard question which turned into a cliché from the amount it is being asked in job interviews. But bear with me a little and let me explain to you what I mean first. I know that this question is common in interviews and I know that a lot of human resources personnel and interviewers ask it. But unfortunately a lot of interviewers as well as interviewees do not know really the background behind it.

When you are asked this question in an interview, the usual answer is something like: Manager, or team leader, or that you would like to move slowly and to take your time to learn…etc. Or any other answer which may convey that you are willing to stay, learn and grow within the company. The interviewer accepts your answer and starts writing something. For you, you feel that you gave an ideal answer which may be true... But only for your employer - not for you.

Where do you see yourself means how you imagine your life style should be in five years. And you should take this question seriously because your future will depend on it. Let me give you an example. Imagine that you are a person who likes to work from his office far more than being on the road. And that you imagine yourself after several years in the job running everything from your office. If this is the case and you applied for a job in sales as an example, it will be the wrong move for you. Because a job in sales will most probably require that you spend more than 50% of your work time on the road visiting customers and building relations.

Or imagine that you see yourself after five years having a beautiful work-life balance, and able to spend more time with your family. In this case, and if you are working in a big multinational company and are willing to work as a manager, then you have to understand that the balance most probably will not happen and that your imagined life will not be fulfilled.

That is why you should first visualize your next five years to find answers for some questions such as: How you are going to work; where; what you are going to wear; the amount of work-life balance; work flexibility; the type of work that you love...etc. before taking any step forward. By doing so, you ensure that you will not waste a lot of time doing something which does not move you forward towards the life that you want.

Every step that you should take in life must be deliberate and taking you one step forward towards the life that you want to live and your long term vision. But since a long term vision or a life vision is sometimes hard to determine and requires time, you can start with a micro-vision which is: Where do you see yourself and how will your life look in five years?

Vision. The Starting Point Of Everything

If you were sitting with some friends and asked each one of them about his or her vision, most probably the answer of most of them will be, "I do not know," or "I never thought about that."

What's Next?

To determine your vision in life and what you want to achieve, you need patience and a lot of trial and error. And trial and error here means going outside your comfort zone and trying things that you have never done before. Things that you feel worried by, just thinking about them - because they seem out of your reach. And this is the point where most people fail because we – as human beings – do not like losing or making errors. We want everything to move perfectly. And if you are willing to go outside of your comfort zone and try new things there is a big probability that there will be errors and failures. And that is why most people prefer to keep doing what they were always doing because they already know how to do it and the probability of failure or error is low.

Going outside of your mastery zone and trying things you have never done before will expose to you any unique talents that you may possess – and you do not know even that they exist. To test this theory let me ask you this question: "Are you able to determine if you are a talented football player or not without trying?" Of course not; you have to try to play first, and after trying several times you will be able to see clearly if you are a talented football player or not. Until the day you ***decide*** to try to play football you will never be able to know if you possess this talent or not. So as you can see it is not about "thinking" that you are a good or bad player, it is about going out to try in order to be decisive.

After discovering something in which you are talented, you need to enhance your skills in relation to this talent. Keep in mind that talents and skills are usually differentiated by a thin layer. Talents are something that you were born with. Something that you are doing better than others by nature. While skills can be enhanced only by deliberate practice and consistency.

Let me again use the same football example to explain. You can try to play football and then discover that you are talented. But even if you possess a super talent you cannot sit at home and say to yourself, "I am ready to play any football game against any team without training." In contrast, you go and train each day in order to master the needed skills and football fundamentals.

When you think about your vision, the best vision that you can have is one which is reached through the utilization of your God-given talents. And that is why it is important for you to try new things, and to discover things about yourself that you never knew existed. And when you discover your talent, think about how you can enhance it, and how can you use it to help yourself and the others around you in order to achieve things you never believed possible.

Passion

Sir Ken Robinson mentioned in his book "The Element" that the sweet spot for anyone is, "When they have discovered their element – the place where the things you love to do and the things that you are good at come together."

To put it in simple terms, if you are passionate about something, you will find yourself willing to do it even if it was for free. You just do it because you enjoy doing it. And passion is really important, because when you will pass through challenges, hard times, and failures, the only thing which will keep you going is your passion about what you are doing and your beliefs.

Please understand me correctly as I do not want to convey a wrong picture to you. Being passionate about something does not mean that you will live each day as if you are living in a dream where the sun is shining and the weather is beautiful and everything is rosy. You will still face issues, challenges, and sometimes you will feel that you do not want to work. But your passion will be the thing which will get you back on track.

So the best scenario which can happen is that you go out there, try new things even if you are going to suck in it or fail until you discover what you are talented in doing. After finding your talent, the question will be, "Are you passionate about it or not? Do you enjoy doing it?" And if the answer is yes, then Bingo. All you need to do afterwards is to deliberately practice and enhance your skills.

Please keep this in your mind. If you kept doing what you are doing then most probably you will keep getting what you are always getting. And if you took the first opportunity which appeared in front of you, and kept working and meeting with almost the same people each day, then you will not discover anything new about yourself and your capabilities. And that is what most people do. They spend their lives doing the same things over and over while surrounded with the same people and mindsets.

Yes – it will be a long journey to discover yourself. Yes – it will take time and focus and trial-and-error to find your vision and what you want to achieve. Yes – it will be full of risks and failures, but it will also be full of successes and fun, and your life is worth every second of this journey. You live your life once and you want to make sure that you achieved your full potential because as Mark Twain once said, "Twenty years from now you will be more disappointed by the things you didn't do than by the ones you did do. So throw off the bowlines. Sail away from the safe harbor. Catch the trade winds in your sails. Explore. Dream. Discover."

Summary Of This Chapter:

1- Always begin with the end in mind. Imagine what you want to achieve and the end result that you want from anything that you are doing; then take consistent actions.

2- Knowing your vision and what you want in life takes time and effort. And you have to be willing to try new things and to fail sometimes in what you are doing.

3- You cannot know if you are talented in something or not without trying it.

4- If you are talented in something, then the question is, "Are you passionate about it or not?" If yes, then you have reached your sweet spot.

5- When you discover your sweet spot, you have to build your skills around it. Start thinking about the skills that you need in order to do great work now and also in the future. And start building these skills. Most importantly, be patient. Building specific skills needs deliberate practice and time.

Supporting Advice:

Think about public or business organizations that you can join. With one search on Google you can find a lot of organizations which can support you. There you will learn a lot. You will meet new people, build your connections and find new opportunities.

Supporting Material:

"The Element" by Sir Ken Robinson.

2 HOW TO REDUCE MY FEAR OF THE FUTURE AND THE FEELING OF BEING INADEQUATE?

"I am not afraid of tomorrow, for I have seen yesterday and I love today." – William Allen White

We all pass through moments of fear no matter who we are, what we look like, what our age is or where we live. The whole game is in minimizing and controlling this fear as much as possible.

We pass through moments of fear of the future and this is because we are uncertain about what we are going to face, or the results that we will reach. We want to make sure that every step we take is correct and will lead to something because we – as human beings – love to feel in control of our lives and our environments. When we feel that we are not in control, we feel afraid.

Small example: If you are about to start a business, and you have a good amount of money as a backup in the bank you will not feel afraid as much as if you are starting with no good backup in the bank. Because when you have backup, you feel in control. You feel that if something bad happens you still have what it takes to steer your life as you want. But if you do not have a good backup in the bank, you start thinking about all possible negative scenarios and the "What if's" keep running through your head. This is because you know that if the business did not work, you do not have good back up in the bank and hence you are not in control anymore.

How To Reduce Fear

As a rule, you can never eliminate fear totally because it is a human instinct. You can only try to reduce it and try to take control over it so that it is not messing up your life. Fear was something that we were born with thousands of years ago in order to help us survive. And the main purpose of fear is to encourage us to take action.

Fear can be reduced only through two things: 1) Taking action and 2) Preparation. I know you were wishing to read something more or something unbelievably extraordinary and complicated. But I am sorry my friend. You cannot run away from the power of preparation and action. And even though preparation as an example seems something easy to do, it is really hard for people to apply. (If you doubt that, then ask yourself, "Why do I leave so many of my important tasks till the last day or minute?")

Let me give you an example. If you have an interview with an employer, the more that you take action and prepare different scenarios, and read about the employer, the more that you will feel relaxed and confident. This is because deep inside of you, you will feel that you did what you have to do and that you do not expect surprises (except in a very minimal range).

The same thing applies if you have a public speech to give or a presentation to present. I am a Public Speaking Champion and one of the services that I offer in my consulting business is Public Speaking Coaching & Consulting. Because of this, a lot of people come to ask me the one million dollar question: "We are scared of speaking in public. How can we eliminate this feeling?" I always used to say, "By practice, practice, practice. The more that you take actions to practice and prepare your speech or presentation, and the more that you give speeches in general, the more calm you will be in front of the audience." Unfortunately most people believe that you will give them an instant cure of fear without any effort from their side.

So if you want to reduce your fear of something, then practice and prepare yourself well. Luckily for you we are living in the era of Google and information technology. There is almost nothing that you cannot find information about on the internet. With a short search you can find any information that you are missing and even find people who passed through the same situation sharing their stories and best practices online.

How To Reduce Your Feeling Of Being Inadequate

Sometimes- especially during your first career years as a fresh graduate – you will find yourself in situations where you feel inadequate. These situations can happen during a presentation to someone from the upper management of your company, a meeting with your boss, or even a discussion with a co-worker. Do not worry – this is normal and we have all passed through the same situation.

This feeling of inadequacy can occur because you feel that your knowledge level about a specific topic is not good enough. So during a meeting with your boss as an example, you may feel inadequate because you do not completely understand the things that he is speaking about, or the expressions that he is using or you may be afraid that he might ask you something and you answer wrongly.

No matter which scenario, here is what I want you to remember: All the people that you see around you passed through the same situation as you. The same start and humble beginnings. But what made them knowledgeable is that they took their time to learn and build their experiences.

Even when you see someone who is in a higher ranking than you. You have to look to him with respect, and try to learn from him if possible. But that does not mean that you have to doubt yourself or be silent when he is around or that you treat him like a living legend. Always remember: This person reached this high position because he took his time and built his network and experience. But who said that if you take your chance you will not be in the same position or even higher in the same period of time or shorter? I am telling you this because it is easy to get impressed by the authority or the rank of the people that you meet in the corporate world. Get impressed yes, but to feel that they are invincible or that it is impossible to reach their position one day is a complete "no-go."

<u>So if you want to pass through this inadequacy phase fast, you have two solutions:</u>

1- **Take actions as much as you can throughout your working day**. When you meet an expert, it is very easy to be overwhelmed by his insights and his right judgements and decisions the majority of the time. But if you ask this expert about the reason why he is making good decisions most of the time, he will answer and tell you, "Through experience" – which he gained in the first place from taking the wrong decisions. That is why actions are very important for you. Take new actions and try new things as much as you can throughout your working day. If these actions were right, you can celebrate and get recognized for them; and if these actions were wrong, then you learned from them and next time you will make the right decisions. Taking the wrong decisions and learning from them are far better than being locked in the cage of fear and doing nothing at all.

2- **Accelerate your learning curve**. When you join a new place, and in order to learn, do not move according to the plans of others. You have to create your own plan. Of course during the first few months you will have some induction courses and introductory meetings with other co-workers and their roles. But that is not enough.

When you join a new company, most probably you will be bombarded with some tasks which need to be finished as soon as possible, which is why they hired you in the first place. Whenever you find the situation more stable, try to learn new things. Ask the co-workers in your team to introduce you to new people in other departments. Start building connections with these people and ask them to sit with you and tell you about what they are doing. Another possibility is to search for the best performers in your department and try to learn from them. As a newcomer to a company, you should target to know new people as much as possible. And this is relatively easy. All you need to do is to smile and to say hello to someone that you do not know when you see him or her beside the coffee machine and you can directly open a discussion.

After you leave work, try to spend 30 to 60 minutes each day reading a book or learning.

If you applied these two tips, I promise you that after just one year, you will be inspired by the amount of knowledge and experience that you have gained. And the best part about it is that you will not even feel it. Because all you did is that you learned small chunks of information consistently for a long period of time. And if your knowledge and experience improve, your feeling of inadequacy will decrease and your confidence level will increase.

What's Next?

Summary Of This Chapter:

1- Fear of the future is usually because of uncertainty. As human beings we love to feel in control of our lives and our environments.

2- The best way to reduce or embrace your fear is through taking action and preparation.

3- At specific moments of your life – especially at the beginning of your career life – you will pass through moments of inadequacy. This is normal and almost all of us passed through the same feelings and scenarios.

4- To reduce your feeling of inadequacy and improve your confidence, you can focus on doing two things: Taking more actions throughout your working day; and accelerating your learning curve.

5- If you take consistent small actions each day, at the end of the year you will be inspired by the amount of things that you have learned or done.

6- Remember: The executives, authorities, and experts that you look up to reached this level because they took their time. So do not underestimate yourself or compare yourself now – as a fresh graduate or as a young professional – with them. These people spent years to build – behind the scenes – what you see now from them in public. **So be patient.**

Supporting Advice:

If you do not have time to read at home, then listen to audiobooks while driving to and from work. You can use a mobile application like Audible to buy the books that you want.

Supporting Material:

"The Compound Effect" by Darren Hardy. This will give you very good insights to how compounding works.

3 HOW TO ATTRACT A GOOD EMPLOYER THROUGH MY CV. AND: WHAT IF I DO NOT HAVE GOOD GRADES OR HUGE EXPERIENCE?

"All successful employers are stalking men who will do the unusual, men who think, men who attract attention by performing more than is expected of them." – Charles M. Schwab

Imagine this situation: You are working in the Human Resources department of a big multinational company. There is a job opening inside a department and the manager working in this department asks you to post this job opening online and start filtering CVs. After 1 month of the job opening you found yourself having around 5000 CVs on your desk. Now you need to filter these CVs in order to send only the valid ones to the department manager, in order to contact only the shortlisted candidates later. How would you feel? And how are you going to do that? Are you going to read all these applications in details including the cover letter, CV, and extra certificates and documents from each applicant?

I believe that even if you were the most motivated employee in the world and you are passionate about your job, you would not read them all in detail. Maybe you would start by reading them thoroughly and in detail but after 10, 20, 50 applications, you would try to find the fastest and easiest way out. And with the first sign that an applicant is not appropriate, you will disqualify his CV. Of course, this job can be far easier if you are working in the Human Resources department of a small local company or if the job opening itself is not that exciting for applicants.

So What Should I Do As An Applicant?

If you are an applicant, you have first to understand the role of the CV. The CV is only a door opener. It does not help you get the job that you want directly, but it makes you pass through the door and take the first step inside. Nothing more; nothing less.

What's Next?

While you are creating your application please keep this sentence in your head "You have one chance to influence someone who does not know you personally in order to convince him or her to contact you and invite you for an interview." This should happen as fast as possible and without you being there to explain to him the background of what is written in the CV or to verify anything. Which simply means that you have to differentiate your CV from the other applicants' CVs from the first moment that he sees it, and to make everything easily understandable and crystal clear.

<u>In order for you to do this, here are some of things that you have to consider while creating your CV in order to give a super impression about yourself:</u>

1- First, break the rules. While building your CV, you will find a lot of people telling you to stick to one CV format. I do not agree with that. You have to differentiate yourself from the others and besides, the CV is supposed to convey your identity. So feel free to browse the internet to check lots of different formats and styles and to choose what is appropriate to you. Just be yourself.

I know that as a fresh graduate this tip of choosing a unique CV format may be hard for you to apply, because the tendency and the social pressure from the others around you to conform and copy their style will be high. But let me tell you this, during your job search journey, you will be rejected lots of times, so why don't you give it a try and try something new and test if it will work or not?

2- During building the CV, applicants need to indicate the role or job position that they filled and state in some bullet points the job description or the tasks that they were doing while working in this position. And here is an opportunity for you to be different.

Let us take an example of a project manager job description. Generally, the role of a project manager is to lead a project team in order to deliver a specific product or service according to the required target time, budget and quality. Now my questions for you are: "If you wrote this in your CV, do you think you are unique? Did you differentiate yourself from other applicants in front of a potential employer?" Definitely not; because 80% of the official tasks of a project manager are well known and usually the same no matter which company you work for, and with one search on Google you can confirm what I am saying. So when you are writing about your tasks or what you did in a specific job role, focus on being unique. Show your potential employer some special achievements. You may think that you do not have any special achievements but sorry to tell you that you are wrong. If you give yourself time to focus and reflect on every stage of your life, you will find achievements. These achievements do not need to be superior or extraordinary, you just need to show that you are unique in any role, job or task that you do.

The best example that can attract the attention of any employer is something that is directly related to either maximizing profit or saving costs. So always search for anything that you uniquely did in any job that you took and try to translate this to savings or profits.

Examples About Unique Achievements That You May Want To Include:

A- You made a technical proposal which resulted in cost savings.

B- You improved the process which made it more efficient and hence resulted in cost savings.

C- You came up with the concept of an idea for a new product or service which generated more revenue for your employer.

D- You are a good presenter and public speaker, so you volunteered to give some training to your colleagues in the company which resulted in improvement in their sales presentations and hence more revenue and profits.

E- You came up with an initiative to build a cross-functional team, in order to map the whole value stream of information flow and communication process between different teams and departments, and to remove waste. This helped in improving communication and increased the work efficiency by removing unnecessary work and documents.

F- Take even this simple example. You made a proposal to change something in your office or company building which resulted in cost savings for the company. This can be outside of your job role or tasks that you do in your daily work, but if it improved the profit or reduced the costs, then employers will look at it as an achievement (and in fact it is).

In any of these examples, the best scenario will be to write a specific amount of savings or profits that the company achieved based on your proposal or initiative. However sometimes you will not be able to determine an exact number. If this is the case, then mention an estimated number (and write that it is estimated in the CV); or do not mention any numbers at all. In the end, writing an achievement or a unique initiative that you took without writing direct savings or profits figures beside it will be better than writing no achievement or unique initiatives at all.

Those are just some examples to refresh your thinking. You do not have to use them but they can show you how to think about the word "achievements". Not only this: If you are already working at a company and reading this book, then you have to start thinking about these examples that I mentioned above and how you can apply any of them – or any other new unique ideas or initiatives that you have – at your workplace.

On the other hand, if you are a fresh graduate directly out of university, you may not have any of the above mentioned examples to include in your CV. Do not worry. Just wait for the next points in this chapter. There are still other ways to enhance your CV other than the special achievements.

3- Which trainings and courses have you taken? Beside each course, write when you took it. The target is to show any person who checks your CV that you are a continuous learner. The worst thing that you can show is that you stopped learning after you graduated or that you took only technical courses related to your job because they were mandatory by your employer. This will not only be a problem for you in the CV; this will also be a problem for you in general.

Never stop learning and educating yourself. Not only during your working hours but also after your working hours. Jack Ma – the founder of Alibaba

Group and whose net worth is estimated to be 23.7 Billion USD – once said, "After work is what determines your future." So how you are going to spend your after work time? Are you going to spend it having fun all the time? Or are you going to create a balance between having fun and learning something new and educating yourself?

4- Which languages do you know? Each language you add to your CV beside your mother tongue language will add value to your CV and will give you a competitive advantage.

5- Are you skilled in using any specific systems, softwares or tools? Mastering or having good knowledge of MS office packet is mandatory in the era in which we are living today. But are you good in any other systems such as SAP, Lotus notes….etc.? And if not, why don't you search for a relevant tool or system and start mastering it?

6- Did you or do you practice any sports? Maybe you were the leader of a sports team? Maybe you achieved a specific ranking in a specific kind of sport? Write it down. Show your skills and also what you have learned from practicing this sport.

7- Have you done any charity work or support? Helping others around you who need help should be one of the goals in your life. Not only to include it in your CV, but because you have a responsibility towards others in this world. Muhammad Ali, the boxing legend and one of my personal role models, used to say, "Service to others is the rent you pay for your room here on earth." So have you paid the rent for your room? Helping others will make you feel better and happy about yourself.

If you consider these seven points, and consider doing these things for the sake of growing yourself even before thinking about writing them in your CV, you will not only build a unique CV, but you will also build a unique life experience, unique life journey and a great character.

<u>Are Good Grades Important? And What If I Do Not Have Good Grades To Include In My Application Or CV?</u>

If you do not have good grades, do not worry: The world is not over. Generally speaking, there are a lot of opinions about this topic. Some experts say that good grades are very important and do really matter; and some say that they do not matter unless you want to apply to academic positions, or Master degrees in some of the top universities such as Harvard, Stanford etc., or some specific major companies and industries like the Management Consulting industry.

For me personally, my advice would be, if you have good grades then this is awesome and good for you, but if you do not have good grades life will still move on. You still can apply and work in some of the biggest companies in the world and do great work. But my statement here does not mean that you can relax and undervalue the importance of studying hard and doing your best to get good grades.

What Happens After Being Invited To An Interview?

The moment you are invited to an interview, the role of the CV is almost over and the rest is on you now. The potential employer invited you because they want to know who you really are. If you do not confirm their first impression that they got about you from your CV, and if you do not convey self-confidence, you will not be considered for the job. And confidence will come only through preparation and rehearsing for the interview; and by doing your research and homework before sitting at the same table with your future employer.

Let me put it this way: The moment you enter the meeting room to make the interview, the focus will be on your character. So you have to show who you really are in an elegant, confident manner and without overselling yourself. You have to convince them that you will add value to their company.

I Got Rejected A Lot Of Times And I Do Not Know Why

If you got rejected lots of times and you do not know why, then you have to run some diagnoses. Were you rejected after sending your CV, or after having a phone interview, or a face-to-face interview?

If you were always rejected after sending your CV or application, then you have to re-check what are you doing wrong in the application or what is wrong in the CV. Maybe the format is not good. Maybe you are not clear enough, or not differentiating yourself from other applicants because you did not show your achievements. Maybe you did not include some of the points that I wrote above or you wrote some of them in your CV but they are looking weak.

No matter what the problem is, it will be most probably in your CV. So here is my recommendation to you: If you are applying continuously and searching for a new job, and for 12 weeks you did not get any interviews, then you have to start examining your CV and finding areas of improvement. Another recommendation which may help you is to contact the employer and the person who sent you the official rejection, and ask them about why you were rejected. If you are going to do this, then you have to convey to them from the beginning that you accept their decision of rejecting you and that you are not negotiating with them, you just want to know what the problem is exactly, so that you can work on fixing it. (Sometimes you get the official rejection from an automated system, and sometimes you get it from the Human Resources person who was responsible to create this job opening, so you can contact him.)

On the other hand, if you were applying and receiving interviews and invitations and after the interviews you are being rejected, then this means that your CV is fine and you have to think about what you are doing wrong in your interview and what is wrong with your strategy. Maybe you did not convey enough confidence. Maybe you were not able to get your message across because you are not that good a communicator. Maybe you were not able to highlight your achievements and sell yourself in the right way. Remember, when you go to the interview, the potential employer does not want you to repeat to him what he just read on your CV. He wants to see your character and for you to give him some insights and background information which were not included in the CV.

As we reach the end of this chapter, you have to keep in mind one important thing. The process of finding an appropriate job is usually a long trial-and-error process. You can try a specific approach in an interview or try to write something new in the CV and test it to see if it works or not. If it works, great. If not, then you have to adjust your strategy and try again.

Finding your dream job will not be easy. You will apply for some positions and get ignored and never receive a feedback. You will get rejected lots of times no matter what your grades are, or your level of experience and certificates. And sometimes you will be one step away from signing a great contract and you will not get it. No matter what happens, do not give up. This is normal. All of us have passed through all these stages. And the good news for you is that you will survive also and reach what you want in the end. You will see the light at the end of the tunnel. Just keep trying and improving yourself.

Summary Of This Chapter:

1- You have to differentiate your application and yourself from the other applicants and make it easier for the Human Resources responsible person who is receiving the applications to pick your application and pass it to the responsible department leader or your future boss.

2- There are seven things that you should consider in your CV. Review them in this chapter.

3- Focus on being unique and adding achievements to your CV. The best achievements that employers like are the ones which are always translated to cost savings or profits.

4- If you do not have good grades, do not worry: You still have the chance to work in some of the biggest companies in the world. And if you doubt what I say, just look around you. I do not think that everyone that you know had superior grades in order to get hired.

5- The CV is just a door opener. As soon as you are invited to an interview you have to show your character and convey confidence. Generally speaking, the only way to feel confident is by preparing and rehearsing for the interview.

6- If you have been rejected a lot of times and you do not know why, you have to make your diagnosis. If you were rejected always after submitting your application and you rarely got an interview, then most probably the problem is your CV. If you got interviews but got rejected afterwards, then it was because you did not influence the interviewer during your meeting with him. Either way, you have to change your strategy.

7- Finding a dream job will not be easy: You will get rejected lots of times. No matter what happens, keep moving forward and do not give up. This is all normal and part of the process.

Supporting Advice:

You can use a lot of internet platforms to build your knowledge. As an example there are a lot of websites which offer online courses such as EDX, Coursera, Khan Academy, Lynda and Udemy. Some of the courses on these platforms have to be paid, and some are free. So you can start building your knowledge while sitting at home.

4 WHICH QUESTIONS SHOULD I EXPECT IN AN INTERVIEW? AND: WHAT CAN I ASK?

"The art and science of asking questions is the source of all knowledge." – Thomas Berger

In one of the previous chapters, I mentioned that we – as human beings – feel afraid of the future because it is unknown and contains a lot of uncertainty for us; and that the best way to reduce this uncertainty and hence our fear is through taking action, good preparation and learning. Within this context you will find in this chapter some of the most common interview questions and how to answer them. Not only this, you will also find some examples of the questions that you may ask your interviewer at the end of the interview.

But before we dive in together and see these questions, I would like us to spend some time adjusting your belief system and preparing you psychologically and mentally before we take a look at the questions. Accordingly, I want you to read the upcoming paragraphs – until we reach the part of the interview questions– and to keep them in your mind before the interview, during the interview and even when you are employed.

Employment is a two way relationship. The employer pays you money and gives you benefits in exchange for your services. They are not giving you this money in the form of salary because they are doing you a favor, or because they are in love with you or even because they want to help you. They are giving you this money in exchange for your services and the value that you bring in. Nothing more; nothing less. So when you are in the interview, do not deal in a way which shows, "Please do me a favor and take me." Or even when you work later in the company, do not neglect asking for your rights just because "the company is paying you salary at the end of the month and that it is good that you are employed in the middle of the fluctuating economy." This is really a pathetic approach which undervalues you – as a human being – and also degrades what you can achieve in your career.

Do you feel attracted towards confident people or not? Do you feel that you want to be around them? Definitely: Yes, almost all of us do. Knowing your value and aiming to reach a win-win situation will show you to be a confident person who knows what he is doing in the interview and hence will gain you more respect in the eye of the interviewer. So please keep this fact in your mind all the time and especially in the interview. The target of the interview is to reach a win-win situation for both you and the employer and not only to get hired "and that's all."

In some cases in life, you may not feel that confident deep inside, or feel that you cannot reach a win-win situation because you do not have negotiation power. Some of the reasons may be because you are a fresh graduate and you want to start earning money after university, plus that you still do not have professional experience, or because you immigrated into another country and you need to find a job because of some financial as well as some legal issues (such as your urgent need for a job to obtain a residence permit and so on). And my answer to you will be: "Yes, I agree with you. It is not always easy to be confident especially in some situations like the ones I just explained. But let me tell you this, being confident – even if you did not get an offer – and leaving a remarkable impression on your interviewer, is far better than showing as not confident and not getting the job anyway. And there is one thing that you have to keep in mind. Being confident does not mean to act in a disrespectful way or to be arrogant. Being confident means that you know your self-worth and based on this you will always – or at least the majority of the time – say your true opinion and point of view and ask for what you deserve because you know that sooner or later you will find the appropriate job for you and that life will not end if you did not get this job that you applied for."

During your career journey, you will find a lot of people around you saying the famous sentence that "everyone can be replaced." When I hear this sentence I get angry because yes, it is true that anyone and even anything can be replaced; but not anything or everyone can give the same value. An employee can be replaced by another employee, but the first employee was finishing his tasks or business agreements in one month while the new one finishes his tasks or agreements in twice the amount of time. In the end both of them achieved the same results but not with the same efficiency and speed. Same for things: A car, a bicycle and an airplane can all achieve the same result – which is to transfer you from one place to another – but each one of them will have different speed, efficiency and limitations; and some of them will make you feel safer and more comfortable while using them than the others.

So do not let any de-motivated or unconfident person trick you and bring you down and convince you of this fake statement. You are unique and different, and you know that you can add value in any place that you join because you trust yourself and your capabilities.

Now let's go to the expected questions that you may be asked in an interview. But please take care: The interviewer may not use exactly the same questions as shown below. He may use different words or sentences, but the meaning will almost be the same as the questions shown in this chapter.

1- Tell us about yourself / What do you want us to know about you?

This is usually the interview opener. And a lot of people start answering this question by directly diving into their CV details. And even though there is nothing wrong with that, it does put you at the same level as any other candidate nominated for the job. Instead, the best approach you can take is to forget about your CV and give something like a very short 30-second elevator pitch about yourself. This elevator pitch is something you have to prepare in advance.

To prepare an elevator pitch which is suitable for a job interview, get a piece of paper and a pen, and write down your biggest strengths or your most important skills; what you love to do; why you are doing it; and how you like to work. After writing these pieces of information connect them all together in one paragraph. After finishing the paragraph, refine and remove the unneeded information until you end up with three to six sentences.

An example can be: "I am a change agent. I love working with teams to dig into details, find waste in the process and make change proposals in order to achieve the required results faster and better; and with cheaper costs."

If you give yourself time to focus and refine your statement you will have a fantastic opening to the interview and this will boost your confidence and give a super impression about you in the first minute.

After giving this 30-second elevator pitch, you can then go back to what you wrote in the CV and start speaking about yourself. When you start speaking about yourself, you can start speaking either about your education until you end up speaking about your current job, or the other way around. It of course depends on where you are now in your career and if you are a fresh graduate who is searching for a job, or if you are already hired and searching for another job.

Generally, my personal opinion is to start speaking about what you are doing now and then go backwards in time. If you have a lot of jobs included in your CV, choose only the relevant ones to speak about; or speak only about your current job and the previous one directly before it and that's all.

If the employer needs more information about the other items in your CV he will ask you. So do not worry.

2- Why do you want to leave your current employer / What can we do to keep you here working with us the longest time possible?

This is a tricky question and the target from it is to know in detail if there are any problems between you and your current employer. A problem in your character, or something that you are searching for that they themselves as a future employer cannot offer you. And the more you answer and give details, the more they will know about your character. So watch out because the more you speak and give details, the more you will become vulnerable to further questions and explanations.

As an example, if you answered this question by saying, "I want to pursue another challenge and grow...etc.," this can be an indication that your current employer is not trying to grow you either because you are not doing well enough or because you are not ready to grow. It can also mean that maybe your employer does not have opportunities now for you to grow. But in the interview, any answer that you give can trigger a lot of thoughts and questions from your interviewer afterwards.

Regarding this question, ideally the best answer should be something which is not related directly to your current employer or triggering new thoughts or questions. Your answer should be focusing on you and what you want or your future employer himself.

An example for an answer which focuses on your potential might look like this: "I believe it is the right time to expand my network, meet new minds (or change the industry), in order to learn more and be challenged by a new way of thinking and doing things." Or you can say, "I wanted to gain the experience of working in a new matrix environment / big multinational company / medium-sized company, with different systems and procedures."

If the employer is very well known and you *truly like* their vision, activities and actions, you can also indicate that. You can say "I respect your vision as a company and would like to be a part of it in the next coming years so that we have the opportunity to grow together." But as I mentioned, if you "truly like" this employer's vision then you can use this reply. If you are not impressed by their vision or if you do not know enough about the company then please do not fake an answer.

Under any circumstances be diplomatic; do not say anything negative about your current employer. And if the interviewer tries to drag you into this zone by making negative assumptions about your current employer and asks you to confirm, then do not give a direct answer. Just smile and say that you prefer not to answer this question because you respect your current employer; and be neutral.

3- Where do you see yourself in five years?

There are a lot of ideal answers to this question. You can say that you see yourself in a managerial role or as a team leader; or that you prefer to keep in the position for which you are applying, for several years until you get the best out of it; or any other answer that you want. It is up to you and how you want to answer this.

But my own opinion is to say something that conveys fairness as well as your expectations. Use a statement like, "I see myself in the place that I deserve based on my efforts and personal development. And I am sure that you will recognize my hard work and progress, and use my skills in the right place – which would serve the company as well as me." This will show that you are seeking fairness. And it will reflect that you are willing to put all your effort and dedication into the job that you will be doing, and in return you expect them to recognize and appreciate that, by growing you and putting you in the place that you really deserve.

<u>Important hint</u>: Please note that there is a huge difference between asking yourself this question to know what you really want as indicated in Chapter 1, and when you receive this question from an interviewer in an interview. When you ask yourself this question as in Chapter 1, you have to be very open and honest with yourself in order to make the right decisions. On the other hand, when you are asked this question in an interview, do not be so open, and give the answer which serves your goal (which is to receive a job offer from this potential employer). Being very honest and open in a job interview may sometimes backfire.

4- What can you add to our company / Why should we hire you?

This question needs a preparation. In an indirect way they are trying to test your confidence level and whether you know your real self-worth or not. They also want to know some of the qualities that you will bring with you.

If you were employed before, it is not enough to say something like "because of my experience", or "because of my previous job experience in this big company" or whatever. You have to break the answer down.

Let us say that you are currently working in the supply chain department of a big multinational automotive company, and that you are in this interview because you want to leave this position and take a new one. You can say "Because I am an expert in the supply chain and I had long experience working in a multinational environment." Or you can say, "Because I am a supply chain expert with a proven track record of working and delivering under pressure in a huge matrix organization, in one of the most demanding industries and some of the most complicated supply chains in the world."

Which one do you prefer?

In answering this question, do not refer only to your current title (if you are already employed) and to your years of experience – and then stop speaking. In fact, you have to break down what you are doing in your current role. Show the challenges that you faced and are still facing in your job and industry because that is what made you who you are today with all your skills and knowledge. Give the employer some insights about the industry, including things and situations that you have survived or problems that you have solved.

5- *What is your biggest strength?*

Please note that if you answered the first question (the "Tell us about yourself" question) as in the way I explained in this book, and started your interview with an elevator pitch which is highlighting your biggest strength, then most probably your interviewer will skip this question because you answered it already.

However, in case you do get asked this question, then just state your biggest strength to them. The interviewer wants to know if you have a good level of self-awareness or not. In case you do not know your strengths in general, then search on the internet for some "employee strengths" examples and see which one fits you. A small research on this question on Google will give you lots of ideas. You can also ask some people that you trust about their own opinion about you and your biggest strengths.

6- What is your biggest achievement?

With this question, the employer wants to know your own definition of the word "achievement" and the one you are most proud of.

Your best achievement does not need to be something superior. It just needs to mean something to you and only you. So do not be ashamed to mention anything that you really feel that you are proud of – no matter how big or small it is – and just be yourself.

7- What is your biggest weakness / What is something that you would like to change in yourself?

This is a tricky question. No matter what your answer will be, do not mention something that is an extreme weakness, or reflecting on your own personal qualities. Moreover, any weakness that you mention should always be accompanied by an action plan. You have to show that you know that there is a weakness – because you are human – but that you did not stop there. You are now working on resolving or improving this weakness by taking courses, coaching or any other thing that you are doing or will do.

If you visit a website like Monster for job search and career advice, you will find them saying: "The best way to handle this question is to minimize the trait and emphasize the positive. Select a trait and come up with a solution to overcome your weakness. Stay away from personal qualities and concentrate more on professional traits. For example: 'I pride myself on being a 'big picture' guy. I have to admit I sometimes miss small details, but I always make sure I have someone who is detail-oriented on my team.'"

8- What do you know about our company?

Before going to any interview, it makes sense to know more about your potential future employer. Some information such as their market position, how long they are in the market, their sales revenue, number of products and industries, how many locations they have worldwide, including manufacturing locations – if they have any – will help you a lot during the interview.

Not only this, you should also check and know more about their vision and values and whether they share your values or not. You should also check the online ex-employees reviews about the company. In these reviews you can see some patterns and what these ex-employees liked or hated the most about the company. This will give you a lot of insights about what to expect.

9- *What is your expected salary?*

There are different scenarios:

A- If you are an experienced professional, and the job post included a salary range, then choose the high end of this range.

B- If you are an experienced professional, and the job post did not include a salary range, then say any number you want as long as it is higher than your current salary (some exclusions to this scenario can be if you are moving to another job with better overall benefits or if there is another strategic reason for you such as less working time or more flexibility...etc.).

C- If you are a fresh graduate and the job post included a salary range, then choose the high end of this range. That does not mean that the employer will accept that, but doing so will give you a better negotiation position in general.

D- If you are a fresh graduate, and the job post did not include a salary range, then do not give an answer. Avoid giving a direct number and let the first call come from the potential employer's side. Moreover, if during the interview they put pressure on you to say, you can answer something such as, "I am sure that you will offer an appropriate package based on my CV, knowledge and potential."

After the interviewers finish asking their questions, most probably they will ask you if you have any questions to ask them. Please do not say "No" and leave. If you leave without questions, you will give the impression that you want to leave as fast as possible because you were not comfortable. Because we – as human beings – tend to avoid the things which make us anxious; or at least we minimize the time we spend on these things. Also, asking questions will show your confidence level and will confirm the message that I told you at the beginning of this chapter: That your relationship with them is a two-way relationship and that they have to convince you to accept their offer just as much as you are trying to convince them that you are the right candidate.

Remember, as much as you want to finish the interviewing process and get the job, the employer also wants to close this job opening and to find someone who will fill the opened position gap.

Some of the questions that you may ask or consider are:

1- *Why is this job opening empty?*

2- *If it was filled by someone and he left, then why did he leave?*

3- *If it is a brand new position, then what is the need for it? There must be an issue/problem/pressure to create this position.*

4- *What does the company want to achieve in the next five years?*

5- *What do you expect from me as part of this short term vision?*

6- *How are you going to develop me? Are there any special development plans inside the company?*

7- *Why do you have not-so-good ex-employees reviews on the internet? Some of your ex-employees wrote negative comments about the company.*

Remark about this question: You might want to ask this question if you saw a lot of negative reviews from former employees online. When you ask this question you have to be prepared that they may ask you, "Why did you come to the interview even though you saw these negative reviews?" In this case you have to explain to them that you do not depend only on what you read online and that you went to this interview to ask and listen to them.

8- *Where is my future supervisor? I would like to speak to him (in case he did not attend the interview).*

This is the most important question of all because your future manager will be the one who either grows you and makes you enjoy the work; or is the one who will make you search for another job. You will spend with him and the team more than you spend at home and you need to make sure that his values and way of thinking are similar to yours and that there is harmony between you and him. Of course in one or two interviews you will not be able to discover all that, but at least you will see some signs which either will make you feel comfortable to join this company or not to. And no matter how much you need a job, please do not underestimate the role and impact of a good manager on you, or the damage that a bad manager can cause to your career. So think carefully.

Summary Of This Chapter:

1- As explained in the last chapter also (and I am repeating it here again so that you remember it very well), we feel fear because the future is unknown and hence there is a lot of uncertainty that we cannot control or influence. And the best way to reduce uncertainty is to take action and to prepare well.

2- Employment is a two-way relationship. The employer is not doing you a favor by hiring you. The employer is hiring you because he believes you are a good fit for the opened position, and the company gives you a salary in return for your services and the value that you add. So clear your mind and be confident and stop looking at it as a favor.

3- The questions discussed in this chapter are some of the most frequent interview questions. If you learn them and prepare yourself well, you will reduce the probability of any surprises at the interview and you will look confident.

4- Do not leave the interview without asking the interviewer some questions. Leaving directly and without asking any questions may show that you just want to get hired, or that you are glad that the interview is finished because you were not feeling comfortable.

5- Make sure that you meet and speak to your future supervisor before you accept the job.

Supporting Advice:

Use the following websites to see the rating of your potential future employer and to get some insights about what is happening inside the company and the company culture.

- Glassdoor
- Great place to work
- Indeed
- Kununu
- Vault
- The Job Crowd

5 WHERE SHOULD I START MY CAREER? OR IN OTHER WORDS: IN WHICH DEPARTMENT?

"What we find is that if you have a goal that is very, very far out, and you approach it in little steps, you start to get there faster. Your mind opens up to the possibilities." – Mae Jemison

A logical question for you while you are searching for a job is: Where to start? Should you work in the Marketing department? Procurement? Or maybe Engineering or Sales? All of us passed through this moment in our lives so here is my best advice for you:

1- Try during your studying years to learn as much as you can about the function of each department and what they do daily. You can do this by asking your friends who are already working. If your friends are fresh graduates, then look within your best friends' network. If a family member (father, mother, brother, sister) of a friend of yours is working in a specific department that you would like to learn about, then ask your friend to introduce you to this family member and ask him or her.

Just make sure that the size of the company that you would like to work at in the future, is similar to the size of the company of the person you are asking. In other words, if you target to work in big multinational companies with over 1 billion dollars of sales revenue and in a specific industry, then choose someone to ask who is working in a similar company conditions and a similar industry.

In the world of business, the size of a company as well as the industry (Automotive, Telecom, IT) can make a huge difference.

2- While studying, take internships as much as you can. If you decided to take several internships, do not take them all in the same department, company or industry. Try as much as possible to take internships in different departments, companies, and industries and create your own diverse portfolio of learning. This will help you a lot later on, when making your own decision about where to start.

Being an intern at a company most probably means that you will be having a lot of daily tasks to do. Most of these tasks will be the ones which the "hired employees" in this department hate to do. Something administrative or which does not need a lot of creativity. You can accept that as long as you are observing what is happening around you and learning as much as you can about how the department works.

Remember, when you are doing an internship, you want to get the maximum knowledge about this department during the 4-6 months that you spend there. So you have to use this opportunity well and not focus only on your daily tasks. Keep your goal in front of you.

3- Make your research on the internet to learn about the important skills required by each department.

4- If you are already studying something that you like, then try to apply for a job which is in the same context as what you are studying.

5- If it happened that you joined a department and found that it was not the best fit for you, then do not lose time and search for a job in another department. Usually finding another job inside the same company and switching internally is easier than applying from outside a company.

6- If you have in your mind a dream company and a dream job that you would like to do in this company but this job is not currently available, then look at your second job preference and try to find an empty position in the same company. Later, you can switch internally. As I said in Point 5, switching internally is far easier and faster than applying from outside.

During studying, most people are willing to finish as fast as possible in order to find a job and start earning money. After graduation, they keep applying to different jobs in different companies and as soon as they are accepted in any of them, they run to take the job and they keep in this job or department the majority of their lives. And this is exactly the problem.

They start working, they earn money and they start spending more and increase their standard of living. They buy new cars and travel around the world. They relocate to bigger apartments or buy houses, and they become more and more dependent on their salaries to the extent that they would never risk losing it, and never try something with an unguaranteed outcome. And later on, if an opportunity came which required them to move to a new department or a new industry, they reject this opportunity because they are not sure if they will succeed or not and they cannot afford to go lower than their current standard of living.

So here is my advice to you, no matter where you start in a company, if you found a chance to move to another department and try something new after minimum two to three years then take it. After two to three years in a job, your learning curve will most probably start to be flat and your momentum will start slowing down, so it will be the perfect opportunity for you to move to another department and gain more insights.

Moving to another department will expand your network, increase your knowledge and give you better exposure. But before making the decision to move to a new department you have to make sure that you know what the benefit is from moving to this department; or in other words why you are doing what you are doing. If moving to this new department will enhance your knowledge and network and will also serve your big vision, then take it. But if it is not serving your big vision then do not do it. Do not be worried or scared to switch.

Take a look and search on the internet for the profiles of top executives. You will discover that the majority of the top executives changed their role or department at least around one to two times during their careers. They do this to have the knowledge of how other departments work and also to have a better exposure and network inside the company.

Summary Of This Chapter:

1- Use the six pieces of advice discussed in this chapter to help you know where to start.

2- Do not be afraid to switch to other departments or job roles to learn more.

3- Most executives in big companies changed their roles or departments one or two times at least.

4- Your deliberate move to another department after at least two to three years of working in the same job will help you gain more insights, expand your network, learn more about the company and its products.

5- If you decided to move to another department, you have to make sure that this move is supporting your end vision or what you want to achieve 30-40 years from now.

Supporting Advice:

Go to a website like LinkedIn or Xing and search for some keywords regarding your future dream vision. As an example if you are willing to be VP Marketing in a big global company in the automotive industry one day, then go to LinkedIn or Xing and write in the search field "VP Marketing BMW". You will find a lot of people profiles. Do this search several times while changing the company name each time. After this, choose three to five profiles and start searching for the patterns within their profiles. Patterns such as: How many job changes did they make? How many companies did they work for? How long did they stay in each job? Which courses did they take? Which degrees do they hold? Look at the common patterns and start creating your own success blueprint and plans.

6 SHOULD I WORK IN A BIG MULTINATIONAL COMPANY OR IN A MEDIUM-SIZED COMPANY?

"Efforts and courage are not enough without purpose and direction."
– John F. Kennedy

The size of the company that you will work for is important for a lot of reasons. We will discuss these reasons in detail in this chapter. The most important things that you have to understand is that choosing the size of the company that you would like to work for is dependent on you, your expectations, career goals and vision. You also need to know that the reasons that we will discuss in this chapter are not all the reasons but the most important ones, at least from my point of view.

As a general rule, there is nothing as "one size fits all". So even though I am trying to generalize my statements about the big and medium-sized companies, in reality this is not 100% accurate because in every industry there are always exceptions.

So we will start now by naming <u>the main advantages and disadvantages of working for a big company:</u>

Main advantages of working for a big company	Main disadvantages of working for a big company
Good name to add to your CV	Slow decisions because the organization is big and lots of approvals needed
Experience in a global matrix environment	The matrix environment can be sometimes hard to handle

Good salary and benefits	Complicated processes and procedures
Job pressure, which is good for your experience and brand as a job seeker	The job pressure can get out of control and harm you
Connections to a huge pool of global employees	

On the other hand, <u>here are the advantages and disadvantages of working for a medium-sized company:</u>

Main advantages of working for a medium-sized company	**Main disadvantages of working for a medium-sized company**
Exposure and direct connection to the upper management	The name of the company will not enhance your CV.
Appropriate work pressure (depending on the industry)	Salaries are not high, with no or small amount of benefits.
Good company culture with better connection between employees across different departments	
Faster decisions and good flexibility to change	
Non-complicated processes	

What's Next?

Now the choice is yours. You have to decide what you are searching for and your direction before making your choice. But no matter what you decide, <u>I want you to remember two things:</u>

1- Again there is nothing called "One size fits all". Some companies can be an exception from the above tables. As an example, you may find a medium-sized company offering a high salary. Or a big company with not so much high pressure due to the industry itself or the job that you will take.

2- There is no mistake that you cannot correct. The problem is when we see the mistake, know what is right and what should be done, and then not do it because of external pressure. So if it happened that you worked in a big multinational company and you found that it is not the right thing for you, then do not hesitate to correct your decision. Do not feel worried or afraid. You were born in this world with specific talents and skills and a lot of potential. But you will never be able to realize this potential if you are not feeling fulfilled or happy deep inside of you. You will never be able to do it if you are dead from inside and alive only from the outside.

<u>Summary Of This Chapter:</u>

1- Before moving forward in your career, you have to choose the size of the company that you would like to work for.

2- The size of the company plays an important role in your development personally and financially.

3- Set your priorities first and compare them with the tables in this chapter to decide your direction.

4- There is nothing called "One size fits all". Each industry is different as well as each company.

5- After being hired, if you felt you made a mistake then correct it. Do not be afraid and do not waste a lot of time.

Supporting Advice:

Take a piece of paper and a pen and go to a place where you can focus. Write down – in sequence – the most important factors that you are searching for in your future employer. For example, you may write that your most important factors are salary, flexibility, and a "healthy" amount of pressure...etc. And based on these factors, choose the size of a company which is optimal for you. But remember, you may not be able to get all the advantages that you are searching for at the same time.

7 WHAT IF I MADE THE WRONG CAREER MOVE OR MADE A WRONG DECISION IN MY LIFE IN GENERAL?

"You are remembered for the rules you break." – Douglas MacArthur

If you made a wrong move – and sooner or later you will – then acknowledge it, learn from it and do not ever feel worried to correct this move.

Nobody can feel your pain, or see what is happening inside your company or career journey, except you. This is a fact no matter how many times you explain to the people around you, or how many times the people around you will tell you that they feel you. So if you see that a job or something that you are doing is not appropriate for you, do not worry about what the others will say; and take corrective action. And with "the others" here I mean your best friend, your girlfriend, boyfriend, wife, husband, father, mother, brother, sister…etc. Also do not be so concerned about how future employers will see it or judge it if this wrong move is indicated in your CV.

This life journey is your own journey and you want to get the best out of it. It is shorter than you think and you definitely do not want to waste your limited time on this earth doing something that you hate to do; or feel unfulfilled because of the judgement of others or because of a salary at the end of each month.

Let me tell you a brief personal story. I opened my first business in Cairo, Egypt when I was a student at the university. I was 22 years old and was full of hopes and dreams and potential. The business had a great start and it was about to expand but later, due to various reasons, I had to close it and with it I closed a chapter of my dreams. Do you think it was easy? Of course not. I saw everything as black and I felt that life would stop.

Several years after closing the company, I graduated with an Engineering Degree and I worked in a big multinational petroleum company. After only two months, I discovered that I was in the wrong place and that I had made a wrong decision. I wanted to correct this decision as fast as possible, so I left the company without even finding another job. Everyone tried to warn me about taking this step. Everyone was telling me that I had to stay in the company as long as they were paying well, or at least to stay until I found a new job – no matter how long the job search would take. I did not listen and I took the step I believed was right and left the company immediately. Because I knew that every extra minute that I spent pushing myself to stay inside the company would only harm my emotional and psychological states. And if my emotional and psychological states are harmed, then I am not able to search for the right job, make the right decisions or feel inner peace.

Later, I found a job as an engineer with Orange (France Telecom) which is one of the leading mobile operators in the world. And to be fair, I had everything a young man can dream of. I had a high starting salary and benefits such as a company car, free cell phone and free calls, and on top of that I had my own apartment. I stayed with the company for several years and then I decided that, for the sake of my vision and fulfillment I wanted to emigrate to another country and pursue an MBA Degree and start studying again. So I decided to emigrate to Germany.

Again, everyone was against it (except just one person I know) and to be fair, maybe they were right because of some reasons such as:

1- It is a totally different culture.

2- I did not speak German (at that time).

3- The risk was very high. And since I was coming from a non-European Union country, I had to freeze 8000 Euro each year in advance in the bank. From these 8000 I was only allowed to spend a specific amount of money each month. And after the MBA was over, I had one year to find a job or else I had to leave the country and go back home and start from scratch.

And even though everyone warned me and told me not to take this action, I took it. I sold all my belongings including my apartment to finance my MBA and started my journey.

During the MBA, I was able to make my Master Thesis and internship at General Motors-Opel, and directly after graduation, I was hired at TE Connectivity (Formerly Tyco Electronics) which is a 12 billion dollar company and the world leader in connectivity. And few years later, I started my private Consulting & Coaching Business.

Before leaving this point here, I want to indicate something to you. I did not have the best grades. In fact, I had a mix of some excellent grades and some bad grades and this did not stop General Motors-Opel from signing a Thesis Contract with me for almost one year; nor did it stop TE Connectivity or Orange or the petroleum company from hiring me.

So as you can see I did everything against the "hidden rules" of our societies <u>which depends on the slogan of "security first"</u>:

1- I opened a private business, and even though things did not go according to plan I did not die.

2- I left a job before finding another one (and with a very low amount of money in the bank). I did not go bankrupt or die from hunger and life did not stop.

3- I worked in some of the biggest companies in the world and industry leaders even though I did not have super grades or had graduated from Harvard or Stanford.

4- I took huge risks and left a secure job with a high salary, and sold my belongings and went to another country whose language I did not speak, to start all over and to be a student again; and in the end I survived and thrived.

So please do not let anything stop you from doing what you believe is right. Break your internal psychological barrier. Choose what you want to do in your life. Feel fulfilled. Take risks. Do not be afraid to fail, and do not let anyone limit you or put you inside a box.

Now, I want to write some few lines to share with you what I learned:

1- Good judgement and decisions come from experience. And experience comes through decisions in general. Some of these decisions will be good and you will win from them, and some will be bad or wrong and you will learn from them. In the end, these experiences and decisions will make you who you are. So do not stop making decisions.

2- The experiences that I gained from my failures (before my successes), and from the risks that I took, and from rising up after falling, and from succeeding after failing, are what encouraged a lot of people around the world to team up with me and to trust me as their advisor, coach, or consultant, and to trust me to walk their life journey with them.

   People want someone beside them who encourages them to do what they thought was impossible, and to unlock their potential. To challenge and to inspire them. And if I had not gathered all these experiences through good and bad decisions and also through actions, nobody would have approached me. So do not be afraid to take risks and actions and to gain as many experiences as you can.

3- The most important thing I learned was that every experience, every success, every failure was nothing but a preparation for another bigger experience coming later in my life. Like a demo test preparing you for a real bigger test which you will not pass if you do not gain the required experience by passing through the demo test. And that I should do my part and then the dots will connect later in my life.

4- I also learned that failure will not kill me and that life will not stop. And that the best thing that you can do is to learn fast, try fast, and even fail fast. Taking action fast, failing and learning from this action is far better than doing nothing.

5- You cannot ask or take the opinion of every person around you. You can listen to anyone you want but in the end you have to make your own decision. Some of the people whose opinion you listened to will never understand your motive; and the majority of them do not have experience related to what you want to do. So why ask them and trust their opinion? In summary, if you want to take advice about investing in the stock market, you should go to real investors and ask them (rather than asking a friend or a family member who just "heard" from a friend that investing is good or bad).

6- Money alone will never make you fulfilled. Fulfillment is about doing something that is meaningful to you.

7- I finally learned that anything you do in life needs time. Nothing happens overnight. Successful people spend years building in the dark, what you see later under the spotlight. How I wish I had found someone to give me this advice when I was starting my first company.

Live your life the way you want. Do not be ever scared to try. Take actions that get you closer towards your big goal and vision. And leave a legacy.

Summary Of This Chapter:

1- If you try new things, you will make bad decisions and you will fall and fall again. This is normal and a part of the process and this is how you will build your experience. The most important thing is to stand up again no matter how many times you fall or make the wrong decisions.

Making decisions, taking actions then failing and learning from these actions is far better from doing nothing at all or from playing it safe in this life and not reaching your full potential.

2- Nobody will feel your fulfillment, pleasure or pain except you. No matter how much you explain and no matter how many people told you that they feel you.

3- If you want to take advice, take it from someone who passed through the same journey or took similar decisions. Do not go to people who have nothing to do with what you are planning to do and ask them their opinions.

4- There is no problem in listening to others around you as long as you make your final decision by yourself. Do not make big decisions only to make others happy.

5- Life will not stop if you fail or make the wrong decision.

6- Money alone will never make you fulfilled. Fulfillment is about doing something that is meaningful to you.

7- Any good thing that you will do will need time. So be patient.

8 IF I AM WORKING INSIDE A COMPANY, WHAT ARE THE MAIN FACTORS THAT CAN HELP ME MOVE UP FASTER WITHIN THE SAME COMPANY?

"Just remember, you can't climb the ladder of success with your hands in your pockets." – Arnold Schwarzenegger.

Some years ago during a training that I was attending, the instructor asked us: "What do you think is the most important factor for career development and progress within an organization?". And he gave us three options:

- Performance.
- Image (Your picture and how you look like in front of the others, and how the people think of you. In three short words: "Your personal brand")
- Exposure (How much you are exposed and known to others within the organization, and especially the real decision-makers)

And he asked every one of us to grab a pen and a paper and to write our opinions as a percentage split between these options. (Ex: 50% Performance, 30% Image, and 20% Exposure or something).

When we finished, he added the scores together to create an average, and then he showed us the results of our estimations as follows:

- 45% of the career progress is based on Performance.
- 35% based on Exposure
- 20% based on Image

However, he indicated that these were almost the normal results that he used to get whenever he held this training with any group. But he also indicated that our estimations and numbers are *not* correct or in other words, does not really reflect what is happening in real life!!

According to Harvey Coleman – President of Coleman Management Consultants, who for the last thirty-five years or more has advised many of the Fortune 100 Corporations – the real numbers are totally different. In his book *"Empowering Yourself: The Organizational Game Revealed"*, the real numbers are as follows:

- 60% of the career progress is based on Exposure
- 30% based on Image
- 10% based on Performance!!

When we saw these results, we were shocked. In the end, who can ever think that only 10% of your career progress is due to your performance!

When was the last time you cared about networking with others outside your team and department? Do you care about your image and how people perceive you or not?

To make it easier for you to visualize what I am talking about, let us look at it from the other way around. When the management of a company is gathered together to make some decisions about the company's future such as succession planning; and whenever somebody of the management nominates a name of a candidate, the other managers will always ask themselves some questions such as:

- Do I know this person personally?
- Do I know what he has done or accomplished?
- Do I know which skill set he has such as presentation skills, leadership, etc.?
- Have I heard others talking about him?
- Is this candidate visible within the organization?

And if the answer for most of the above questions is "No", then most probably you know already how this will affect this candidate's career progress or in other words "nomination" for a leading position.

Do not interpret my words here wrong. I am not saying that you have to be lazy or to stop working smartly or hard. All that I mean is if you are an ambitious person, and willing to climb the career ladder and you were thinking that this can only be done through your performance, then you have to rethink your strategy and to focus on your exposure and your image as well.

Moving up the career ladder requires selling yourself. Selling yourself means that you consider yourself metaphorically as a product. Now, let us say that you are the owner of the best product in the world and that you are willing to sell it. Are you able to sell it if the people and potential buyers do not know about it? Another reasonable question is, are you able to sell a product if it does not fulfill the customer's needs? That is exactly what you have to understand in order to move up.

In order to sell yourself, you must be able to understand how the decision-makers in your organization think, or in other words "find their frequency". When you switch on the radio, you have to find the right frequency first before you are able to listen to the channel that you want and eventually your favorite radio program. And that is exactly what you need to do.

You need to find their thinking frequency, and then align yourself with their areas of focus, and position yourself in an appealing way which conveys how can you fulfill their wants and needs, and solve a problem for them.

But how to do this? <u>As a starting point you can focus on the following:</u>

1- What is their vision, what are the short-term and long-term goals they are striving to achieve? Are you focusing on the same goals or are you focusing on things which you "think" are important?

<u>Additional tip</u>: Do not focus only on your team or department goals. Look at the big picture.

2- What are the important business terms and ratios they are using and which ones are important to them? Are you using the same terms and ratios – in other words their language – while you are speaking to any of them?

The purpose here is to find an area of commonality between your goals and language and theirs. Having common things with someone is the first step to resonating and forming a strong connection with them in general. So after you answer the above two questions, you have to make sure that anything you do is aligned with the points above.

But is this enough? No. This is only the first half of the equation.

The other half is to know the "rules of the game". Any company usually has a specific matrix which the decision-makers and upper management use for succession planning of higher positions. Do you know this decision matrix? Most probably you do not know it, but you "think" you know it.

As an example: Let us say that you are a manager in "XYZ" department, and you are working really hard and aiming for your next career move. You built a great reputation and you got yourself exposed to the upper management and decision-makers within your department. Suddenly, a "Senior Manager" position in your department opens, and since you are living in the fantasy "Lala land", you are almost 99% sure that you will be selected for this position and you start preparing yourself for the day of the announcement.

Finally, the day of the announcement comes, and you discover that they have chosen another person – who in your opinion is less qualified than you – and you find yourself waking up to a nightmare in the real world. You start wondering what happened, and after some research you discover that the decision matrix for the level of this position requires that all vice presidents of the other six departments approve your move or promotion, and since you were isolated and caring only about great work and exposure within your department, you lost the chance against another (perhaps less qualified) colleague who was more exposed within your department as well as outside your department.

How to know the decision matrix within your organization? Simple. One of the ways is just to go and ask. Stop guessing and asking colleagues at the same level as you, and go directly and hear it from the mouth of the head of your department or one of the upper management with whom you have a good connection. They will be glad to tell you because it is not a military secret. It is just unusual that people care about knowing the matrix and that is why nobody usually asks the right questions.

Knowing the decision matrix for the succession planning and higher positions, is crucial for your career development within any company. And when you pack this knowledge with the ability to read the decision-makers' minds and being on the same frequency in order to know how to position yourself, your career progress will be unstoppable.

Summary Of This Chapter:

1- To move up the career ladder inside a company, you need more than just good performance. Good performance alone will not move you up or will move you up until a certain level only.

2- In any company that you work for, having the right image and a good exposure to the decision-makers will pave your way to the top.

3- You have to know the decision matrix of the company that you work for. Who are the key decision-makers as well as how do they choose candidates during their succession planning meetings.

4- You have to sell yourself. And in order to sell yourself you have to tune in to the same frequency of your upper management and decision-makers. Know what they are searching for and what they really want; and speak their language.

Supporting Advice:

Know who the main decision-makers are inside your Company and try to connect with them. Let them know your name and who you are. If you are not able to reach them personally, then choose some of the people that they hang out with and build connections with these people. You have to make it easier for them to choose you for a future position, and to do that they have to know you – or at least someone that they trust has to know you.

Supporting Material:

"Empowering Yourself: The Organizational Game Revealed" by Harvey Coleman.

9 HOW CAN I ACCELERATE MY CAREER PROGRESS IN GENERAL AND ALONG WITH IT EARN MORE MONEY?

"When you are going up the corporate ladder or the government ladder, you have to take some risk." – Condoleezza Rice

Several years ago during an event, I found myself sitting beside a Chief Supply Chain Officer of one of the major corporations in the world. The funny thing is that several days before the event – when I knew that he was going to be one of the attendees – I was checking his CV on the internet and I had some questions. I was hoping to get the chance to speak to him later in the event for some minutes.

After he sat down beside me and I introduced myself to him, <u>a discussion started</u>:

Me: You know, I am really glad that we are sitting beside each other and having this dialogue because I have a question that I was always willing to ask to one of the C-suite Executives. I saw in your résumé on the internet that you worked in different functional areas such as Marketing, Supply Chain, Procurement...etc., and also at different global locations around the world. Through observation, I saw the majority of high-level executives following the same trend or pattern. They paved their way to the top by working abroad and also in different functional areas and departments. My question is: "Did you plan all of these relocations and hopping between departments or did it all come by coincidence?"

Him: Well Mohamed, some of them came by coincidence and the others were planned. You usually start your way dreaming big and having a vision to fulfill. Based on this vision you plan your moves and actions accordingly. It will happen of course that, along the way, some opportunities to move to other departments or to work abroad may pop up. You can accept these opportunities as long as they are not contradicting with your end target and vision.

After this event, I spent several years trying to find an answer to the question, "What is the fastest way for an employee to reach the top?". And even though I never found a "one size fits all" answer, I did mainly find a common pattern between the majority of the people who reached the top fast and are now <u>leading organizations:</u>

1- **They changed their roles several times through their career journey.**

There are several benefits to changing your role or job through your career:

a- It makes you understand the function of other departments and teams, and gives you a sense of the big picture. In other words, it allows you to see the process end-to-end. When this happens, you can understand how your colleagues in other areas think; you can understand their feelings and the pressure that they are passing through, as well as their main milestones and targets that they usually focus on.

This will lead you to make better decisions while having a better "buy-in" from other departments within your organization because you care for their goals and know how they think. Better decisions supported with better buy-in from other colleagues means better results and hence creating a better brand for yourself.

b- Another benefit for changing your role is that it expands your influence and exposure within your organization. Instead of spending the majority of your life in one department and influencing only the people around you, you can have the chance to influence more people and expose yourself to more decision-makers. This will accelerate your career development process.

2- **They took overseas assignments.**

CEO Coach Debra Benton - the CEO of Benton Management Resources, Inc and the author of "CEO Material" – mentioned in her book: "If you do not go out into the whole world literally and figuratively, you will look ignorant, be ill informed and be unprepared when the world comes to you (which it will) in the form of customers, vendors, peers, and bosses. A good thing to learn is global awareness. You get a fresh perspective, are less prejudicial about race/culture, and you think more broadly". And one of the ways to achieve this is through taking foreign assignments.

Anne Fisher – a contributor to Fortune Magazine online edition – highlighted the importance of having an assignment abroad and its role in your career development in an article that she published in Fortune Magazine online in 2011: "Those globetrotting managers may have an edge over their stay-at-home peers. International experience is 'more frequently becoming a prerequisite' for top-level executive jobs, notes Dr. Mansour Javidan, Executive Director at Najafi Global Mindset Institute."

"Recent studies suggest he's right," she continues. "Executive development consultants Healthy Companies International, whose clients include Intel, Northrop Grumman, Johnson & Johnson, and Boeing, examined the career paths of C-level managers at Fortune 100 companies and found that more than 7 out of 10 have held management jobs in foreign climes. That's up from fewer than 5 in 10 a decade ago. 'In many big companies now, you need at least one substantial international assignment if you want to climb the executive ladder,' says Bruce Raines, CEO of New York City executive search firm Raines International."

But is there a chance that taking an assignment abroad can backfire or that the management at the headquarters might forget about you?

Anne quoted in her article the following answer from Bruce Raines: "As for your fear that you'll be 'out of sight, out of mind' at headquarters, Raines says you needn't worry too much: 'Before the Internet, people sent overseas were isolated. Now, with Skype, video conferencing, and all the other technology that's available, you're never really out of touch.' That's not to say that going abroad poses no risks to your career. You say that your division head has mentioned sending you abroad for 'a year or two.' Raines says one hazard he has often seen arises when that year or two turns into five or six. This happens a lot, he says. 'By the time you do get back, after a long stint abroad, the organization has changed so that there's no comparable job for you. So you either take a step-down or leave the company.' To be on the safe side, Raines urges you not to take an overseas assignment 'unless it is one that will help your career even if you end up leaving your current employer.'"

3- They changed their employer several times.

Jeanne Meister – an HR advisor and Contributor on Forbes – wrote in one of her articles: "For newly minted college graduates, job-hopping can speed career advancement. According to a paper out of the St. Olaf College's Sociology Department entitled 'Hiring, Promotion, and Progress: Millennials' Expectations in the Workplace,' changing jobs and getting a promotion in the process allows Gen Y employees (employees born in the 80's and 90's) to avoid the "dues paying" that can trap workers in a painfully slow ascent up the corporate ladder.'"

She added, "Job hopping can also lead to greater job fulfillment, which is more important to Gen Y workers than it was to any previous generation: A 2012 survey by Net Impact found that 88 percent of workers considered "positive culture" important or essential to their dream job, and 86 percent said the same for work they found "interesting." Job-hopping helps workers reach both of these goals, because it means trying out a variety of roles and workplaces while learning new skills along the way."

I remember personally that, during my career, one of the fastest and extraordinary job hoppings that I witnessed was the case of a senior manager at a big corporation, who transferred to another big multinational company on a Director level. But after only three months of his transfer, his old company contacted him again to get him back because they "suddenly discovered" that they need his services urgently. Moreover, to convince him to return back they offered him a Vice President position. (Take care that this is an extreme example of job hopping and never the norm.)

One point to keep in consideration is that sometimes too much job hopping in your CV can backfire. So make sure that the changes that you make are always purposeful and aligned with your end vision.

Job hopping does not only accelerate your career, but it has also another benefit as it guarantees you better money besides fast career development.

According to Cameron Keng – who practiced taxation for clients such as Goldman Sachs, Deutsche Bank and Pfizer at PwC as well as KPMG – and his article in Forbes: "Employees Who Stay In Companies Longer Than Two Years Get Paid 50% Less."

He mentioned in his article that "The average raise an employee can expect in 2014 is 3%. Even the most underperforming employee can expect a 1.3% raise. The best performers can hope for a 4.5% raise. But, the inflation rate is currently 2.1% calculated based on the Consumer Price Index published by the Bureau of Labor Statistics. This means that your raise is actually less than 1%. This is probably sobering enough to make you reach for a drink."

"In 2014, the average employee is going to earn less than a 1% raise and there is very little that we can do to change management's decision. But, we can decide whether we want to stay at a company that is going to give us a raise for less than 1%. The average raise an employee receives for leaving is between a 10% to 20% increase in salary. Obviously, there are extreme cases where people receive upwards of 50%, but this depends on each person's individual circumstances and industries."

He also moved further in his article by asking, "Why are people who jump ship rewarded, when loyal employees are punished for their dedication? The answer is simple. Recessions allow businesses to freeze their payroll and decrease salaries of the newly hired based on "market trends." These reactions to the recession are understandable, but the problem is that these reactions were meant to be "temporary." Instead, they have become the "norm" in the marketplace. More importantly, we have all become used to hearing about "3% raises" and we have accepted it as the new 'norm'. […]

The world is desperate for skilled labor and companies around the globe are starving for talent. Companies can tout technology replacing labor, but it is only exacerbating the global shortage of human capital and skilled workers. This means that we as employees are positioned better than ever to leverage our abilities for increased pay."

Summary Of This Chapter:

1- Changing your employer, changing your job role, and taking overseas assignments are the fastest ways to help you climb the career ladder and earn more money sooner.

2- Overseas roles give you global exposure and allow you to learn how to integrate and interact with other cultures. And this is something which is required in big organizations.

3- Employees who stay in companies longer than two years usually get paid 50% less.

4- Changing your job role makes you understand the function of other departments and teams, and also expands your influence.

Supporting Advice:

Look around you and identify one of the executives in your organization that you believe is doing an outstanding work and who – from your own point of view – reached the top of the career ladder fast. After you identify him or her, check his résumé or employment history to see which factors from the above-mentioned ones he applied during his career journey. After doing this, ask yourself: "What is the best next step in my career journey which is aligned with my end vision?"

Supporting Material:

"CEO Material" by Debra Benton.

10 When To Switch My Job Or Department, And: When To Leave The Whole Company?

"Quitting is not giving up, it's choosing to focus your attention on something more important. Quitting is not losing confidence, it's realizing that there are more valuable ways you can spend your time. Quitting is not making excuses, it's learning to be more productive, efficient and effective instead. Quitting is letting go of things (or people) that are sucking the life out of you so you can do more things that will bring you strength." - Osayi Emokpae Lasisi, Impossible Is Stupid

During your career, you will face a lot of challenges and problems. Some of them may require you to change your department and search for another job internally and other ones will require you to look ahead and start searching for a job outside the company.

Of course, there are also some common sense reasons why you may want to leave your company such as: Another company is offering you a better salary, or that you found a higher position in another company and this new position will make you go one step closer towards your end goal, and so on.

But truly speaking, I do not count these reasons as the most important ones which can really and severely push you to search for another company. In the end, these problems can still be solved. Yes, another company may offer you a better salary but who told you that you cannot raise your salary at your current employer. Or another company is offering you a higher position, but maybe after an open discussion with your employer – and if they really need you – they can also offer you a better position. These are common problems which might be solved with some negotiations between you and your current employer. So I will not discuss them here. Instead, I will focus mainly on the severe problems that require an immediate action from you.

Below, are some problems or red flags that you may spot inside your company. If you spot one or any of them, then you should start thinking about moving to another company:

1- If you do not see a clear vision and direction from the upper management.

2- If you do not feel that your opinion is valued or that your voice is heard.

3- If you do not feel that the upper management is connected to the employees, and you start hearing the word "them" (about the upper management) from your colleagues.

4- If the company culture is not the right one for you. You can easily spot the wrong culture because it will contain a mix between toxic people with wrong behaviors, and good people with the right behaviors.

You may say "Yes, but this mix is available in almost every company". And I will tell you that you are correct, but the difference is in the management reaction to this wrong behavior. If your company rewards or keeps a person with a wrong behavior only because he is a good performer, then your company culture is not good. Because sooner or later the behavior of this toxic person will push others to be selfish and focus only on themselves and their own benefits instead of the whole company or team. Not only this, but also teamwork will decrease and later some of the best employees will leave.

If you pass through one or some of these four problems in your current company, then you must start searching for another one. Waiting at your current company because you have become used to it and because you know the people and systems, will not take you anywhere and will delay your career.

You may ask and say, "But do all problems require that I leave the company? Or should I move to another internal job or department?" And the answer is, "No, you do not necessarily need to leave the company. You may want to stay at your current company and merely move to another department or job internally".

This is the case in the following examples:

1- If you are always in conflict with your manager and you do not like each other and he does not like your way of doing things.

2- If you are always overloaded with work and this is always putting you under high negative pressure. And no matter how much you complain, no one cares.

3- You do not see clearly where you are going in your current job. You always try to explore and know what your next move is, but your manager is always asking you to be patient or he does not give you a clear answer.

4- If the values of the team that you are working in are not matching yours. As an example, if one of your main values is to "deal with your colleagues as a team" and your colleagues in the department or team are not dealing with each other as a "real" team, then you will never feel happy no matter how much you earn.

5- If you feel unfulfilled by doing what you are doing. Or if you feel that your learning curve is not getting higher anymore.

6- If you asked yourself, "Why I am doing what I am doing?" and you found yourself answering and saying, "Only because of the money".

7- If your work is never appreciated no matter how much effort you put into it.

If you pass through one or more of these problems, then it is enough at the beginning to start searching for another internal job only. Keep in mind that these are not all the reasons. There may be other reasons also for you to leave your department or your company but I only wrote here what I believe to be the most important.

In the end, taking the decision to leave your department or the company depends on you, what you want to reach, and of course your personal judgement.

Summary Of This Chapter:

1- During your career journey, you will face a lot of challenges and problems. Some of these problems may require you to leave the job or department while staying within the same company; and other problems may require that you start searching for another company.

2- There are four main problems or red flags that should indicate to you to start thinking about moving to another company.

3- In the main, there are seven problems or red flags that should indicate to you to start thinking about moving to another department or job role.

4- More money or a higher position are not severe problems which may lead you to leave your company. Because there is still a chance that you could reach a compromise or a solution with your current employer about these issues.

I wish you all the best of luck in your future decisions and an inspiring career journey where you reach your full potential and feel fulfilled.

ABOUT THE AUTHOR

Mohamed Hanbal is the President of Hanbal Consulting- a Consulting & Coaching Company located in Germany. He is an Entrepreneur, University lecturer at DHBW Mannheim, Leadership & Performance Expert with extensive years of experience gained through working in some of the biggest Companies in the world such as Orange, General Motors and TE Connectivity.

He is also the south west Germany Champion of Public Speaking 2015 and one of the top 10 finalists in the North, Middle and East Europe Championship of Public Speaking 2015.

Mohamed is holding an Engineering degree from the Arab Academy for Science, Technology & Maritime Transport, as well as an MBA degree in International Business Consulting from Offenburg University of Applied Sciences.

What's Next?

www.ingramcontent.com/pod-product-compliance
Lightning Source LLC
Chambersburg PA
CBHW061201180526
45170CB00002B/907